MW01419486

Everything About You

Poems Inspired By Love And Loss

Dan Kraus

First Edition

NEWMAN SPRINGS PUBLISHING
320 Broad Street
Red Bank, NJ 07701

First originally published by Newman Springs Publishing 2024

ISBN 979-8-89061-698-2 (Paperback)
ISBN 979-8-89308-582-2 (Hardcover)
ISBN 979-8-89061-699-9 (Digital)

Printed in the United States of America

To one person that changed my life—a person that when I was around them, I didn't have a care in the world. I was exactly where I was supposed to be. I also share it with you in hopes that maybe one person that is going through the same experience and knows that they are not alone reads this. While some of these poems are very personal and only pertain to one other person, I hope you enjoy these silly little quips and wish you all the best!

Why Do I Love You?

You asked me once, “Why do you love me?”
I’ve thought long about it and hope that you see

I love you because of the way you make me feel
I am where I should be, it’s a feeling so real

I have lived a life where I always felt out of place
But with you by my side, that is not the case

You make me feel something that I have never felt
A special kind of bond that makes my heart melt

I love everything about you and all that we do
I love that feeling of home wherever I’m at with you

I love going out with you or taking a trip
I love the game we play called Just the Tip

I love your kids, your family, and your friends
I love the kindness and love that your heart sends

You can ask me this now or in a year or two
My answer will be the same when you ask why I love you!

Six Months

It's been six months
since I had to leave our home
It feels like forever now
That you decided to be on your own

Are you happier now
Since you don't need to worry
There's no guilt now
There's no reason to hurry

Stay out all night
Or sit at home by yourself
It's you who decides
What books you take from the shelf

I realize more now
That I did a few things
I pushed you away
Now my broken heart sings

It's a song about our love
And how I still want you
But that day doesn't come
And there's nothing I can do

I write these silly words
I think they send a strong message
But they may never even be read
I can't recover from the wreckage

I'll keep on writing for myself
Until my heart sings a new song
But I know deep in my heart
That our love wasn't wrong

For me, I had found
Exactly what I was looking for
This was it for me
I could not want any more

For you, though
Your search will continue
You are looking for a love
That you feel is within you

I understand now
that it isn't with me
No matter my love
I cannot make it be

I hope you find again
All that we had
I'll remember my time with you
And for that I'll be glad

Waves

I'll sit by myself
Or maybe go for a drive
It hits me quickly
It lasts for a minute or five

The feeling of loss
The feeling of missing
Remembering us
The hugging and kissing

These things hit me in waves
They make my stomach turn
They tear through my body
And make my broken heart burn

Small things do the most damage
They remind me of you all the time
And make me sad to think
We're not together, that's the crime

Will you miss me
The way I miss you?
Will winter nights
Make you want me too?

I'll wait a lifetime
It's the only thing I can do
And let these waves hit me
Each time with something new

Let Her Go

"You have to let her go"
"You have to let her be"
I hear it from everyone
But I'm just too blind to see

I thought this love was strong
I thought it would last forever
We had everything we wanted
The two of us facing life together

But life takes a turn sometimes
It's when you least expect it
It's like what loves does
Every time you neglect it

So we live worlds apart now
As if we never met
And go on our separate ways
But it's you I'll never forget!

After Five Years

After five years
It makes me sick to hear goodbyes
After five years
Seeing your texts still gives me butterflies

After five years
I'm still in love with you
After five years
I wish you loved me too

After five years
You've finally had enough
After five years
The breakup is still so tough

After five years
I wish I could just stop time
After five years
I still want to call you mine

After five years
I have to face life without you
After five years
I'm lost, with nothing left to do

So I'll go on hurting
Fighting back the tears
Because my love for you hasn't faded
Even after five years

Falling Out of Love

I suppose it happens every day
People don't feel it anymore
They fall out of love with the other
And watch as their love walks out the door

Do they regret it at all?
Do they ever feel pain?
Do they think about the other person?
Or to them, was it all a game?

The one still doing the loving
Is the one hurt most of all
Their heart ripped out of their body
When they try, all they do is fall

The other maybe moves on
They maybe get on with their life
While the jolted one keeps feeling
The sharp pain caused by their knife

But life does move on
It never stops for this
No matter the pain and the loss
Or missing their touch or their kiss

So things will get better
All I can do is pray
That smiles come back to my face
I can only hope to see the day!

Texts

I stare at the phone
Waiting for the vibration
Every day I wait
Waiting for your salutation

Just a simple hello
Or an "I'm checking on you"
Whatever words you use
To let me know we're not through

It's a pain that doesn't end
But seems to linger forever
A longing that doesn't die
Waiting for the day that we're together

Will fall bring that day
When the leaves turn different colors
Or maybe the winter nights?
Have you searching for a lover?

Whatever the path you take
I hope it leads back to me
So we can continue our amazing life
Because my dreams won't let me be

Pictures

All our pictures are the only things now
All the memories live there, packed in somehow

Each one tells a story if you listen closely
It's the story of our life and what fun, mostly

But that's all I have now since you went away
So I reminisce and look at them every day

Hoping that they bring peace to my tired soul
So I can smile again, at least that's my goal

I may never reach it because of how I feel
How I miss the love we had, something so real

I've lost you forever, your heart will go to another
And maybe I get a chance one day to show I won't smother

Until that day, these pictures will have to suffice
And for this love lost, I paid a hefty price

Wish It So

I can't wish it so because if I could
I'd wish you were by me, like you should

I can close my eyes or open them wide
I can show my feelings, or they can hide

No matter what I choose, it doesn't change the fact
That nothing I do can wish you back

I can go out for the night and say I moved on
Or sit at my place and wonder why you're gone

I can say a prayer every day, or I can dream
No matter, you aren't coming back, it seems

As I wish for you back, you're busy with whatever
Meeting new people, away from me forever

I'll carry my memory of you no matter where I go
And dream that maybe you also want to wish it so

From the Beginning

We knew from the beginning there was something we shared
We were drawn to each other from the beginning we cared

There were a lot of obstacles, and each time, we overcame
The silly notes and meeting up and our cute little nicknames

Our young love grew, it grew stronger each day
We had to be together, there was no other way

With us there was something, we were in love from the beginning
Soon enough everyone knew it was your heart I was winning

We spent our time together, we didn't want anything more
With everything going on around us, we knew our love was pure

But now we are alone, we have to recreate what we found
Go out into this cold world and hope it's the same this time around

I'll tell you right now for me, there won't be another
That makes me feel like you do that can turn my winter to summer

I hope in our time apart that you, too, can see
with all the guys in the world, they will not love you like me

So I let you go into the world to find what you're looking for
And when you don't find it, just open
your heart and unlock the door

Because you know I'll be standing on the other side
My love will show through, and my happy heart won't hide

Why Do I Write?

People make fun
They ask me why I write
When it's all fruitless
Since you're out of sight
My answer is the same
No matter time or place
It helps me get through
The horrible times that I face
I write in hopes
That there is one special verse
That makes you realize
Our love is a blessing, not a curse
I write for myself
It's what I like to do
I'll share them at times
Hoping that another likes them too
Who knows what the future holds?
All I know for sure
That if I don't write these words
I would miss you even more

What Do You Do?

Questions bounce around in my head
I'm wondering just where you are for the night
Are you with friends or family?
Maybe it's a guy, maybe it's Mr. Right

The questions wrestle around in my head
But which one do I answer first?
There are so many answers it could be
My head could seriously burst

What do you do with yourself each night?
What fun are you out having without me?
Do you see me next to you at all anymore?
Or was it so bad that now we can never be?

What do you do the first thing in the day?
Do you wake, like I do, and think of the other?
Do you reach out to the other side of the bed
But instead of me, my place was taken by another?

It's such a shame that we got to this point
That we aren't hanging out, having our fun
Instead, silence has replaced all our smiles
And I can't think of a reason why, not even one

So another day comes and goes
And it's followed by a long night too
All I can do is lie in bed, staring blankly
My thoughts turn to wondering, *What do you do?*

Two Thoughts

I wake each morning
With two thoughts on my mind
The first is of you
And our little bind
The second thought is
What words will spill out
To describe you perfectly
And leave you with no doubt
As to my love for you
And how I miss you so
And wish your love for me still flourished
Just like so many days ago
We can still have this
For the rest of our days
Going on trips or staying home
There are so many ways
We have so much to do
But when will we start?
Will you give me the chance
To put love back in your heart?
I can only hope the day will come
The love comes back, the love we sought
And it fills my head again
With more than two thoughts

Sorry

To say I'm sorry
Would not be enough
I handled this wrongly
Because it was so tough
I was controlling
And I didn't believe
You would always only want me
And that you would never leave
And so it's over now
I have to learn to live without you
But funnily enough
I think another thing is true
That you will come back
Once you've finished your fun
Living by yourself all summer
Until your adventures are done
I'm sorry for sure
That I acted so wrong
I didn't want to let you go
I thought our love was so strong
And I still believe
That our love will endure
And we'll be together once again
And I won't want anymore

Let It Be

I've heard all the instructions
I need to move on, need to let it be
I'm making a mess of things still
When all you want is to be free

I cannot apologize enough to you
If you could just forgive me
And work on us again
So our life can continue to be

It's the best thing
That's ever happened in my life
Meeting you and falling in love
I believe it even through all the strife

You said it yourself
That a break can be a good thing
And we'll come back stronger
And make your beautiful heart sing

So again
Just so you see
It's hard for me to let it go
It's hard to just let it be

Crossing a Bridge

I crossed over a bridge
and saw the water rushing by underneath
Whirlpools of water swirled
and formed little foamy wreaths

I thought about that water
Does it even know where it's going?
Or does it just follow its path
without ever really knowing?

Does the water know
what's around every corner and turn?
Or does it just stay within its banks
passing all the flowers and ferns?

Love, to me
is exactly like that water below
blindly following a path
not knowing where it will flow

It will start as something small
maybe just a tiny trickle
But it will grab everything in its way
because it's not very fickle

And when it gets moving
like that water, it's not done
until the river is consumed by the ocean
and the two become one

Everything about You

I love your eyes, your hair, and even your skin
I love your kiss, your touch, and the dresses you're in

I love our home, our trips, and holding your hand
I love going to the bar just to listen to a band

I love grilling our food or snacking on chips
I love just talking or putting my hands on your hips

I love the soccer and baseball, just going to the game
I love looking in your eyes and speaking your name

I love the word *babe* and all the things that we share
I love being with you, that's when I don't have a care

I love our life together and everything that we do
Babe, I hope you know I love everything about you

Follow Your Heart

I search for the nights, but the days never end
I write words in a letter that I never mean to send

Our love burns so brightly deep in my heart
But you are so far away, that's the worst part

"Always follow your heart and never your head"
Songs tell you that, at least that's what they've said

I can only hope your anger finally gets replaced
As you remember all the challenges we faced

We've overcome each one and always pulled through
This is just one more challenge to overcome too

Kissing and hugging and holding you tight
By your side, to me that feels just right

We have so much to do, we just have to start
But it only begins when you follow your heart!

I Won't Forget You

If you think I'll move on, I probably won't
If you think I'll forget you, ha, please don't

If you think all my love for you has left my heart
Or I'm all happy and smiling the time we're apart

I'm neither of those that are listed above
I'm sad and lonely since you fell out of love

You've moved on, as they say, you're no longer mine
But the love we shared, I don't think you'll find

It is a love that lasts way longer than our romance
It's unconditional, it's a special love if we give it a chance

So I'll live my life, because that's how it has to be
And I'll go through the day hoping you don't forget about me

All the Advice

Everyone smiles as they say, "Get on with your life"
But how, when my heart has been stabbed by a knife

A knife so sharp it ripped my heart right out
Then tore it apart and left no doubt?

It's hard to listen, everyone has some advice
I know their intentions, they're just trying to be nice

But this is a feeling that I've never felt before
A strong connection I feel down to my core

I listen intently as they spew their suggestion
Nodding my head as if listening, and then I question

How can the advice that people love to give
Pertain to my situation and the way I live?

Because people's advice is always the same
"Move on with your life please, forget her name"

But I can't forget her name, her face, or her smell
It runs through my veins, it's like living in hell

Because she didn't chose me, she made up her mind
She'll live her life her way, but it's not very kind

Was I Wrong?

Did I see something in you that was never there?
Was I wrong to think we were going somewhere?

All the great memories that we've made through the years
Are like old books on a shelf that told of lies and fears

All the love we shared, I shudder to think
They were fleeting moments gone in a blink

I thought we made it, that we lived a great life
But it was gone one day, and that cuts like a knife

I couldn't have been wrong, it was there in plain sight
A genuine love of two people that felt just right

We had something special, most people have told me
But at the end of this, was it a lonely life that you sold me?

So I'll travel alone now, I'll walk my own way
Learn lessons that life teaches, and hope for a new day

One Call

Can I tell you everything
in just a single call?

If I don't open my mouth
have I told you anything at all?

If words don't rush past my lips
and thoughts don't enter my mind

Have I lost something special
that I was never meant to find?

You've come into my life now
and I want so badly to hold you tight

But with those feelings comes doubt
If I'm not there, are you all right?

Will someone eventually
get to feel what I feel?

Will they smell your hair and skin
and think it's a really big deal?

With love comes loss, and I ask
"Why does it have to be so?"

Because this love's loss will be huge
since you finally let me go

Things We Do

Cutting grass, laundry, and even the mail
You can do those things and not even fail

Grocery runs, even grilling on the deck
Give me a chance, please, what the heck

Taking our trips and going out to the bars
You know all the places, I consider them ours

Taking our walks and exploring new places
Find all the parks, making sure to touch all the bases

I list all these things to help you remember
Our cruise is still booked in the month of December

Why do it alone when you have a partner to take?
And we can then still enjoy the love that we make

Trips to the lake, we can still do that too
Because this is a list of the things that we do

The Phone Buzzes

The phone buzzes, and I look to the screen
Searching for you name, but that's not how it's been

I get a text, and my broken heart beats so quickly
it's never you anymore, making my stomach so sickly

I'll wait for the day, for that call or one text
And then feel sick to read what might be next

It could be that you have found the right one
And you thought about it and you're still done

I want so badly to talk to you, to see your face
And go with you to our favorite place

To watch TV and just lie around in bed
But we can't because of something I said

Or it's you going through your midlife crisis
But we're in this together, my help should entice us

So I hope you reach out, and we can discuss this
Until then, I pray someday the phone buzzes

One Thousand Years

Will the hurt ever stop, will I stop feeling the pain?
It's a feeling of numbness, from my toes to my brain

How many years of torture, someone ripping out my heart,
How many years of this, I'll bet one thousand to start

All the days run together, but time moves so slow
One thousand years seem so long, how many more to go?

A feeling so strong only comes around once or twice
You should never let it go, that feeling, so nice

To go from on top of the world, to sinking so low
Try pulling myself up, try to stretch and grow

One thousand is a big number, do I have that many tears?
That's a long time to cry, for one thousand years!

Never Lose You Again

I want you in my life
You just have to say when
And if I'm given the chance
I'll never lose you again
We have something special
Everyone can see it
We can have an amazing life
We just have to believe it
Holding hands together
As we travel these roads
I can read these to you daily
My little poems and odes
We can have lazy Sundays
As long as you're mine
Or we'll go to Grafton
And sing "Sweet Caroline"
We can make this life
As great as it can be
I don't want to lose you
Please don't lose me

How Many Days?

How many days need to pass before it feels like forever?
How many days to stop missing you? The answer is never

How many lonely nights does there have to be
When all I can think about is you here with me?

My mind starts to wonder in the brightness of light
about things that can only be in the darkness of night

I move through the day as tears stream down my face
Stumbling my way through, I feel out of place

Do you think of me as the days go by?
Tears filling your eyes as you begin to cry

Will your eyes meet mine in the same way
As the times they did before you went away?

How can so close seem like so far?
How can I stop wondering where you are?

I want to tell you these things that I feel way down deep
But something stops me, and I just cry myself to sleep

My World Since You've Gone

My world came crashing down all around me
I felt it changing but was too blind to see

The blue sky now is a strange kind of gray
The sun hangs there but doesn't brighten my day

Nights linger around for far too long
Sleep doesn't come, people ask what's wrong

But they really don't want to hear all my trouble
They're just sad when they realize we're not a couple

Will I get another chance? Will you miss me a bunch?
We'll be happy, I think, but it's only a hunch

It's a long, lonely summer without you by my side
I just want to jump in my car and go for a ride

Aimlessly driving around to different places
Maybe stopping somewhere just to see all new faces

Because my friends see my eyes as withdrawn
that's how I cope in my world since you've gone!

Break

I heard you say *break*, and my heart volunteered
Yes, it broke the moment that you disappeared

You hold the key to make it whole once again
I don't know if that day will come, I don't know when

A summer apart shouldn't turn into a life
So I'll wait out the time of the anger, the strife

Will you realize that what we have is called love
And it's bigger than both of us, that it comes from above?

We share a bond that we grew through the years
Through the laughter and trouble and through the tears

To me, our love is as solid as a rock
I hope you feel it as well and turn back the clock

So my heart volunteered, I think it was a mistake
Because it will hurt for as long as we're on a break

Fighting Demons

I'm fighting demons, these are ones you can't see
They're things I've done and stories about me

But they're hard to fight because they always shift
Like pans of gold, though through each one I sift

Look for the truth and why those stories aren't real
Or if I did do one, that's not how I really feel

These demons are crafty, each one tells a tale
Sowing seeds of doubt down to the last detail

They make you think, not good thoughts but bad
The misery and torture, these thoughts make you sad

But turn it around, think of all the smiles that were made
Don't listen to the demons, be strong, not afraid

Our love is there, it's ours for the taking
The fun to be had, the memories we're making

Take that trip with me, I can only beg and plead
Start with a weekend away, it's all the time that we need

Out of Place

I sit around at places
Places I don't want to be
I sit around with people
People that I don't want to see

I found something in you
Where I finally found my place
I was where I should be
Looking at your beautiful face

Going out for dinner
Even out for the night
Or just staying at home
With you it's just right

But for hidden reasons
That I simply can't see
You decided no more
You didn't want me

I won't believe that you want to go out
And try to duplicate this
I won't believe that this is over
Because I'm the one you miss

Days are turning to weeks
And then they turn to years
And we aren't any closer to talking
You're ready to move on, it appears

And maybe I fade into oblivion
I disappear without a trace
And then I'll go on living
Like before, out of place

My Home Is with You

You flew to Savannah, and I stayed behind
Laughing and having fun, but I hope that you find

What you miss most isn't the traveling
It's the love we share, which feels like its unraveling

But it's a strong bond, and I truly believe
we can work through this so I don't have to leave

I wrote about our house, but that isn't at all right
Because without you there, it just not as bright

So Savannah, Chicago, even San Diego too
I have realized one thing: my home is with you!

All I've Done

Even if you wanted
You probably wouldn't come back
I drove you away
I guess it was the confidence I lack

I've done so many things
To drive you away
Talked to too many people
And believed what they say

I should have trusted
That you were always being honest
I blamed and accused
I should have done just as I promised

I beg and plead for you
To forgive and take me back
Holding on to me and my love
Turning my sky blue instead of black

I'm sorry I drove you away
In a heartbeat, you were gone
And I regret it every day
I'm sorry for all the things I have done

Drama

I did this to us, I created the drama
I'm sorry to your kids, who call you Mama

I'm old enough, I should have known better
Now all I can do is keep writing these letters

With you, as I've said, I'm where I want to be
By your side, always having you here with me

I understand now what I did so wrong
Believe me, I've heard it in word and song

You're done, finished, you don't want any more
You've turned the page, you've closed the door

But to me, is this a period or is it a comma?
Because I promise there will not be any more drama

I Have to Believe

I just have to believe
I have to trust what you're doing
I have to believe
That in this time away, your love is renewing

I have to believe
That a break can be great
I have to believe
That we'll go on another date

I have to believe
That the world we'll still see
I have to believe
Because my thoughts won't let me be

I have to believe
That this break won't be long
I have to believe
Because I know our love is strong

And when you come back
I never want you to leave
So I close my eyes and wish
Because I just have to believe

Nobody but You

"You Are the Woman" and "Lovesong" by the Cure
Listen to these songs and know that I'm sure

You know Old Dominion sings "Some People Do"
A song of forgiveness, and that's what I beg of you

"She's Out of My Life" and the Eagles' "Wasted Time"
I'd be rich if for every love song, I got a dime

If I do get the chance to see Morgan Wallen
We can listen to "Last Night," and in love we'll be fallin'

You love "I Prayed for You," a song from the heart
It's about me in your life if you let me play the part

I could go on listing more, each with great meaning
I only hope if you listen, letting me in
your life is how you'll be leaning

"Sometimes" by Erasure and even "Love Me Do"
All say the same, babe: I want "Nobody But You"

The Perfect Song

I wish I could write the perfect song for you
I wish you'd hear it and know exactly what to do

Or write the perfect poem with words from my heart
About how I miss you the whole time we're apart

My story is told in every song that I hear
They sing of love gone wrong, of sadness and fear

Afraid they lost their love and can't be complete
Or afraid it won't be the same with anyone they meet

Songs tell of pain and sing of loss so real
And with each one, I think that's exactly how I feel

I'll keep listening for instructions on how to right my wrong
And I'll keep searching for words to write that perfect song

There's No Giving Up

I'm not giving up, there's too much at stake
A lifetime of fun, so many memories to make

I'll beg you and beg you, "Please take me back"
One last chance for us, it's not love that we lack

You say you were all in one time before
Please take me back and be all in once more

You will not regret it, not even for a second
I will run back to you whenever you beckon

I won't give up, that's a promise I'll keep
For a lifetime of fun and our love that runs deep!

Waiting in Vain

Waiting in vain for a single call
Sitting in silence for anything at all

The walls are collapsing, sinking in a big hole
Grasping and clutching, spiraling out of control

A fool to think something could come of this
But there was so much emotion in one little kiss

It's hard to believe, but could this be love's spell?
Like an old friend's return, one you knew so well

No, I won't let this take control of me
Then love wraps its arms around, and I can't break free

Holding on so tightly for one little sign
Putting everything on hold until I know you're mine

We can't make it be, we'll pay too high a cost
But do I have a choice since my heart I've lost?

The words pour out of my head once again
And I pray that tomorrow won't bring the end

Poems

Will I run out of words, or can I keep writing?
Will you understand that I don't want to keep fighting?

I wrote these poems, they come from the heart
Flowing out of my head the whole time we're apart

Poems help me cope, they're for you and me
Telling of our love and how it could be

Maybe one hits home, and it makes you think
I made you mad, put our love on the brink

Maybe one will show you this is all so real
Our life together and how you make me feel

So read the poems if you like, I'll keep writing more
It's how I hang on for now until you reopen the door!

Throughout the Day

I walk throughout the day and look at the clock
I imagine what you are doing with each ticktock

Maybe you're home or working out at the gym
Maybe at work, driving home as the sun starts to dim

You could be on a date or out with family and friends
Or tanning at a beach, where the ocean never ends

Concerts are another thing that you like to do
But who are you going with if I'm not with you?

It kills me to think of what drove us apart
We loved each other so much, you held my heart

This fall starts back soccer, all three girls playing
Road trips, of course, but where are you staying?

I hope I cross your mind in some little way
And I hope you think of me throughout the day

All In

I may see your face, but then again, I may not
You say you look a mess, but I think you look hot

We talk, and when we do, tears form in your eyes
But "all in" means there's no time for goodbyes

So take your time if you must, it's the right thing to do
But know at the end of the day, I'll still want you

"All in," for me, is being with you and seeing you happy
"All in," for me, is my love for you, I know it sounds sappy

"All in," for you, means you have to take a chance
"All in," for you, means "step up and join in the dance"

So think about us, and think about the good times we've had
Look at pictures of us and smile, you won't be sad

Please, babe, it's a small chance you will take
For a lifetime of happiness, a great couple we make

All in Again

"All in" means forgiveness for a wrong that's been done
"All in" is working through problems, it can't just be all fun

"All in" is loving someone even when you feel you just can't
"All in" is talking about life even when you just want to rant

"All in" is listening and giving your all
"All in" is picking up the phone for one more call

"All in" is something that's earned with time
It's not just given without reason or rhyme

"All in" is loving for both when one doesn't feel it
"All in" is not giving up, they just try to heal it

"All in" is forever, and it's there for the taking
"All in" is our life together, it's memories we're making

Looking at My Phone

I look at my phone
Even more than I should
Waiting for a text
If only you would

But day after day
I keep waiting in vain
Not sure why I wait
With nothing to gain

Except the thought
That we'll be together once more
It's a matter of waiting it out
Babe, please just open the door

You said to me before
That you just wanted a break
You couldn't ask me to wait
But I held out my heart for you to take

You took my heart
Maybe you hid it under a stone
One thing's for sure
I won't find it by looking at my phone

Home Is Where the Heart Is

They say home is where the heart is, and I believe it to be true
But for me, it isn't so because my heart is with you

Our life, our fun
Our time, our sun

We should shine brightly, we should light up the sky
But the clouds darkened it all, and I don't know why

I would change things around if I'm given the chance
We can work on the word *can* instead of *can't*s

My love for you won't fade like the setting of the sun
No, it grows inside my heart after each day is done

So take the summer, I just hope not a lifetime
Because one of these days will turn out to be the right time

Because for me, home and heart are the same
And they're intertwined in love's little game

Broken Heart

There are songs that sing of broken hearts
Stories tell of lost love, of stops and restarts

The words they use, they sing with such passion
They sing of forgiveness, hearts filled with compassion

I listen to these stories and start to think
They sing about me and of how low I sink

The songs sing of a heart that breaks and dies
And I feel each one as wet tears fill my eyes

Do these songs help you heal? Do they help at all?
Do they help pick you up right after you fall?

Maybe they're there to help get a new start
And show that you don't have to die with a broken heart

Trust

I thought I'd write what I feel in my heart
I trust you completely, that has to be a start

I want so badly for you to give me a chance
To prove my trust, but stubborn is your stance

You said I changed, which may be true
But what hasn't changed is my love for you

So if people change, they can change back
I just need you to believe, get our love on track

You know what we have is unbelievably strong
I believe with all my heart I just can't be wrong

You're afraid that maybe I'll go back on my word
But you explained the issues, and, babe, I heard

If no one is in the picture for you
Then trust when I say we can work this through

We can have it all, an amazing life
Carly Pearce, Old Dominion, and Matt Rife

Start with a date to rebuild your trust
But having you in my life, that's always been a must

Do You Remember?

Remember Helen's? The place where we'd meet
Or Vegas and zip-lining down Fremont Street?

We spun on the wheel and got drunk on free booze
I had found you and felt I couldn't lose

Next was COVID-19 and hanging on St. Pat's
Small crowds but exactly happy where I was at

Next up was our trip to Mexico in 2020
And we'd also hit up Florida and Miami

We went to San Antone to celebrate my day
July, Branson with the kids, I wouldn't have it another way

The balloon races were next, we saw them at the park
And stayed out forever and got home after dark

To Denver for Jimmy Buffet, we saw at the Rock
Pikes Peak and Breckinridge, man, did we walk

We traveled to see a great concert in Austin
We've been many places, but we missed Boston

Back to Vegas twice in 2022
There's so many places to go just with you

We went back to Mexico, this time with the girls
And our cruise was fun, let's give it another whirl

All the soccer trips we've taken through the years
There have been a lot of trips and too many beers

But these are the things that we have done, you and me
Please think about them as you struggle to see

That we fit together, our life has been great
It starts once again if you'll agree to a date

How Are You?

Every day people ask, "So how are you?"
I smile and lie and say I'm making it through

But they read my sad face and see the pain in my eyes
Because instead of speaking truth, I'm telling all lies

If the truth came out, I'd say my heart is broken
Torn out from inside by words that were spoken

I had found in you, everything I was looking for
My search was over, I couldn't want any more

With you, I was exactly where I needed to be
And for the first time ever, I clearly could see

You are my one, bringing a smile to my face
Happy together, no matter time or place

So I smile and lie, what else can I do
When asked the question, "So how are you?"

We Had Made It

Any way that you look at this
We had made it
Even though logically
We should have forbade it

We were happy each day
Hanging wherever together
Life had become easy
It was as light as a feather

For years it was so
But was something else brewing?
What I thought we were building
Were you working at undoing?

Did it build up over months
Or for years was it coming?
At some point, did you decide
A different beat you were drumming?

I am sorry for all of this
If I didn't see it happening
It could have been hell for you
And all the things you were imagining

I understand now when I look back
There was some pain I caused you
You felt second sometimes
And doubts that my love was true

I can only beg you please
If given that chance
Let me prove my love to you
And prove this powerful romance

Coming Home

It's in the darkness of the sky
and the stillness of the trees

It's in the coldness of the air
and the weakness of my knees

It's in the knots in my stomach
and the lump in my throat

It's in the ache of my heart
and in the words that I wrote

It's the feeling of emptiness
and of being alone

It's in all these things
until you finally come home

Mending

It was too good to be true, the dream had to end
How long, I wonder, until my heart starts to mend

A broken heart is tricky, you just feel like dying
Lying in bed all day, holding your pillow and crying

Mending your heart will just take awhile
People tell you that, and I just have to smile

Little do they know that this hurt can never heal
It will always be broken, that's just the way I feel

You find the one, the girl that makes you complete
It's once in a lifetime and luck that you meet

But sometimes it takes more than just love
It takes a belief, something dreams are made of

So this pain will go on because it's never ending
Until you come back, my heart won't be mending!

Strained

I strain to find different words
To express how I'm feeling
I feel I've written so many poems
I can stack them floor to ceiling

Some days, all the words
Just flow through from my mind
Other days, the words don't come
They're very hard to find

No matter the words I use
The meaning is all the same
They talk of loss and heartache
Framed all under love's name

The words I use talk of anger,
Love, pain from deep in my heart
Asking for forgiveness from you
And learning from this as a start

So read if you like
Or you may just delete
I'm not asking for anything
Except to make my life complete

How Do You Do It?

How do you do it, how do you get through the day?
Do you look at your phone to text but have nothing to say?

How do you go through the week and not give us a thought
Or take weeks away with all the trips that you've bought?

How do you not remember all that we promised?
To love each other, and it was sealed with a kiss

We would talk things through as one, and we'd never part
How do you look at our pictures and not know you have my heart?

We were taking on the world, we'd sail through life
Maybe no ring, but I considered you my wife

And I was your everything in those days gone by
How do you do it, be all in but not give us a try?

Tears

I have a lot of tears built up inside me
I expect them to rush out, pain won't let it be

Gone forever, that's how it's starting to feel
The sadness in my heart is all still too real

A love taken because of jealousy and fear
I've lost it all, everything I hold dear

So tears stain my face, they fall down like rain
Each one drops down, maybe flushing my pain

But I hold out hope that you will come back
So my sky will turn blue instead of black

Tears are replaced again with smiles and laughter
Together again, living happily ever after

Drive

I drive the same roads
But my car doesn't make the same turns
It drives straight by our house
All while my heart aches and burns

"It's not healthy," they say
"You've got to move on"
"She doesn't love you anymore"
"She's already gone"

I should listen to the advice
Plenty of people have been here before
And had their heart broken
But each eventually found more

But what they found in their life
Did it make them feel great
Or did they just cope each day
And trust what happened was fate?

So the years pile up
Will it take four or five
To not have my heart break
Each time by our house I drive?

Hope

You give me some hope, a little each day
It's in the actions you do and not the words that you say

My hope is that you think often and want us back
My hope is to get our love back on track

I hope each day brings us closer to each other
With the time away, I hope you don't find another

I hope that you still think of me every day
And you miss me in every possible way

I hope to see you smile once again
And hold you in my arms like it has been

I hope to lie in our bed with you
And cuddle after the long day is through

I hope we can be together once more
And hoping that you haven't closed the door

My hope is to hear the words "I love you" in time
And know again you are all in and all mine!

Sitting at a Park

I'm sitting at a park, and I turn to the sky
Contemplating life, mine is wrong, but why?

In my mind, I could never do anything wrong
But reality is tuned to a different song

I worry, and I overthink to much
Overreacting to the slightest touch

My brain never stops when it starts its journey
I know my thoughts are wrong, that doesn't deter me

By yourself, your mind tells a strange kind of story
It grabs a hold of you, it twisted and tore me

I turn to the sky as light turns to dark
And can't remember why I'm sitting at a park

Meaningless

Words written on paper that no one reads
Words trying to send a message that no one needs

Are they meaningless, or do they have a meaning
Depends on who sees the words and if they are reading

Or do they get crumpled up and thrown away
In a dump somewhere, never to see light of day

I'd like to think that they serve a purpose
Maybe to calm someone that appears to be nervous

Or helps another in their time of need
Find comfort from the words that they read

And maybe when you think that all is lost
The words find a home after all and aren't tossed.

All I Want to Do

All I want to do is see your face smiling at me
See that love in your eyes, just like it used to be

How we lit up a room just by being there
How we walked through life without a care

If we just try once again, it could be that way
Maybe not right now but, hopefully, someday

We'll travel the world, we'll be the talk of the town
You'll always be happy because I won't let you down

Come back when you're ready, you know I'll be here
I'm a phone call away, I'm really that near

Tell you I'm in love and only want you
It's a simple life because that's all I want to do

Crazy

The texts I usually send now seem crazy
The thoughts in my head are very hazy

I was out yesterday and just want to tell you
I want to call or text because that's just what we do

I'm where I'm supposed to be when we are together
By your side, having fun, it's all sunny weather

It doesn't matter if it's three days or three years
Hell, thirty years from now, it certainly appears

That I'll be loving you still, but where will you be?
In our bed, at our house, and lying next to me

I'm so sorry that I put us in this place
You want to move on maybe and have your space

But think of us often and all the love we share
I've let you go, but I will always be there

Waiting on the day, a Sunday so lazy
When maybe these words don't sound so crazy

Rides to Work

I'm looking back on our life
Remembering all that we've done
I thought we had made it
My heart you had won

We go together so well
We have such great times
Can we continue this trip?
If so, I won't stop the rhymes

The rides to and from work
Were my most favorite of all
I listened to all your stories
There are too many to recall

It was our time in that car
Where I got to hear and ponder
Your passion and dedication
I always listened in wonder

My phone holds our history
A reminder of all that we've done
But it's those rides to and from work
That's where my heart you had won

The Biggest Problem

The biggest problem since you've gone
Is that you are busy, and I don't fill your mind
On the other hand, with all my time
You fill my brain, and my thoughts are not kind

I think of all that we did right up until the end
Is there a chance to get you back in my life?
Can we smile again like before?
Can you come back and be like my wife?

You say that you can't
Find the love back in your heart
But I think you can if we try
We just have to find time to start

We have something special
We'll find it again the deeper we dig
And as everyone can see
Our problem isn't that big

Confidence

I was never quite confident that I could ever have you
That is why I act like I act and do the things that I do

Of all the things we share, it's hard to know what is true
Place yourself in my spot, on the other foot, put the shoe

I thought that time was fading, and I had to show you how I felt
I made a move without you, I took a shot from the belt

You may never know just how sorry I will be
I changed into something I liked, you changed, but I didn't see

The person you became for me was someone you didn't like
I have to live with that and without you for the rest of my life

I know you think you knew me, and I think you still do
I really am the person you fell for, and in time I can show you

Right now I have to rely on your memories to bring you back to me
I made the mistakes and lost the thing that makes me happy

So if you decide one day that I am the person you need
I'm just a phone call away, I'll come running indeed

Thoughts on Paper

I have thoughts running through my head all day
But will better thoughts be with me tomorrow?
If I hear a great phrase or a lyric from a song
Would it be okay to write it, okay to borrow?

Tomorrow might come
And I have no thoughts at all
Or as time marches on
And summer changes to fall

Will my memories of us start to fade?
Will you move on with someone new?
No one knows what tomorrow brings
What it won't bring is another love that's true

I miscalculated our relationship
I thought it was so solid
But I questioned something in us
I asked a question, that's all I did

Now all I have are these yesterdays
Memories of our life, you and me
Who knows about the future
Because tomorrow is yet to be

I'm Sorry

"I'm sorry, but I don't want to try again"
Those words ring in my head every now and then

I hear them in the morning and again at night
It's a message you sent to help me see the light

"I just need a break" is another phrase too
At the time, I thought it was what you must do

But as time passes like a stranger on the street
I'm understanding it's a stranger I'll never meet

So living separate lives is all that remains
Out of sight and thought just to ease the pain

"I'm sorry" is also what I've said to you
I've said it ever since we've been through

I thought those words supposedly heal
But for you, I guess, that's not how you feel

No words can fix this nor a cute little phrase
Actions won't help either or singing your praise

So I'm sorry for this has to be the start
Please accept it, and let's stop living apart

How Can It Be?

I wake in the morning and can't believe it's real
A hole in my heart, that's just the way I feel

I'm not driving to our house at the end of the day
Or laying my head on my pillow, it's just not that way

How can this be, how can we go from love to hate?
How can we not be going out, getting ready for our date?

For me, everything happened so fast
Out of your life, I was gone in a flash

But I'm hopeful that there comes a day
That you realize us together is the best way

We can continue our journey, travel our road
I'll love you forever, our story yet to be told

Thinking Back

Thinking back on our life and all that we've shared
Vegas was our first place, and we really cared

Next was Florida, where I karaoked with Pat
Lying on the beach, do you remember all that?

We went back to Florida, this time further south
We had fun, it was the people we could do without

There are so many places, I can't list them all
Nashville, Kentucky, South Carolina in the fall

We went back to Vegas and then off to Mexico
We partied at the lake where you loved to go

Puerto Vallarta was where they sang to you at dinner
Our Decembers were busy in the middle of the winter

We crossed that long bridge, it was so dreadful
Got caked in mud, none of this is regretful

Traveling back to Vegas with your girls in tow
We have so much fun no matter where we go

Onto our great cruise where we saw it all
Traveled to places and different ports of call

Whether we travel with family or we travel alone
We love time with each other because it always feels like home

Words and Actions

They say that through time, actions are louder than words
And if you are listening to your heart,
then I'm sure that you've heard

All our actions point to a not-talked-about fact
Our love isn't over, based on how we act

The way you cuddle up to me when we lie down to rest
Or grab my hand tightly and place it under your breast

Holding on to me, especially when I'm snoring
Or stealing a kiss from me on a sleepy Tuesday morning

Dinner and dancing and drinks at the bar
We do these things still because that's who we are

Dropping you off or picking you up when you're done
To me, that's the greatest, it makes the day more fun

You say that you're trying, I believe it to be true
But I'll love for the both of us because that's just what I do

My actions cost me everything for now
I hope your actions can forgive me somehow

You tell me to move on, but I just haven't heard
Because the love we share shines through action and word

Feelings

Your feelings have changed, and maybe that's true
But my feelings haven't because I still love you

And this will still be true in five years or ten
And if you find it's true for you, just say when

Because I will wait, I have no choice
My feelings are my only voice

I say these words so that maybe you'll hear
And want this again, please make it so dear

I moved out, and you moved on
Because you say your feelings are gone

I'm hoping that none of what you say is true
And let me show you through actions that I do

For now, though, my head is still reeling
Because you've lost that loving feeling

Taking on the World

I used to think I could do anything, but now I'm not so sure
I could take on the world, but it's not so anymore

It seems for me, I need someone beside me
To travel these roads, I need someone to guide me

In you I had found that, a true life partner
Someone to teach me, someone who's smarter

We had such a good thing that I want once more
But you needed a break, I hope this will help you be sure

We belong with each other, our hearts beat as one
If you just say the word, I won't walk back, I'll run

My Home

No matter where I go or how far I roam
I'll always consider your house my home

You've taken that away, but you kept my heart
My hope is to be back, and dating is a start

We'll go to dinners, the movies, or even a show
You'll remember the love, and then you'll know

We have so much left to do around the house
Deck, basement, I'm in, and I have no doubts

Give me the chance to show the love that's missing
And we go back to all the hugging and kissing

I look around the house, and everything is ours
Mulch in the beds, even planting some flowers

The closets, TVs, all the food on the shelves
Most everything here, we did ourselves

We can go back to the place that we so love
Holding each other tightly and doing all the above

Please forgive my careless words and don't say shalom
And then say yes to us and let me back in my home

The Good in Me

The good in me far outweighs the bad
And yes, I'll do things that may make you mad

But forgiving to move forward is the only way
Can you give it a try? What do you say?

Look to your heart, it will speak the truth
See the love like our relationship was in its youth

It's there for the taking if we really try
And make our love great without saying goodbye

The crazy words that spilled from my lips
Won't ever be heard again, there will be no slips

Concentrate on us and how great we can be
If you do, I think you'll see the good in me

You Changed Me

When I say you changed me, it's all for the good
You made me happy, I loved you as best as I could

The things I did, it was for no one else but you
Dinners and laundry and taking Kate to school

Taking trips, loving you, and making you smile
Those things can continue maybe after a while

I changed because of how you made me feel
I look back at our life, it was all so real.

You pushed me away, saying you wanted a break
We're in different stages of life, but we're not, for Pete's sake

You have two kids almost the same ages as mine
They'll be living their own lives, it's just a matter of time

So Kate is your younger one, and that may be true
Even though not biological, I consider her mine too

Going on soccer trips or teen parties at the pool
Union Station and lunches, she thought that was cool

So you see, both our life stages are the same
This is life for us, and it's our own little game

Hanging On

I'm hanging on to the thought that we'll be together
Maybe you'll miss me in the fall and cold weather

I still can't wrap my head around being apart
I live in this condo, but you have my heart

Hang on to my heart and give it back one day
I'll hold yours also and protect it, if I may

I hope you hang on to the thought of our love
Mine won't fade, it's what our dreams are made of

We go together, we have such a good time
You can still have your life, and I'll have mine

But our life together, surely, you must see
That even at the end, we still made each other happy!

Believe me when I say that you have all my trust
If you just try once more, I swear I'll adjust

You Wanted This

Is this what you wanted? To live worlds apart?
Does this make you happier since I had to depart?

Will our lives be better since you sent me away?
Will the sun ever shine again even if just for a day?

U2 sings of not finding what they are looking for
And the same for you, I guess, you are looking for more

For me, my journey ended when you entered my life
I had everything I wanted except seeing Matt Rife

But now I have tickets to see his show
The only question now is "Will you go?"

Let's go on a date, let's find each other again
As I've said in poems before, you just have to say when

And if it's not this show that you attend with me
Maybe it's Old Dominion or the cruise, just make it be

Or I'll wait a lonely lifetime and keep hoping we will
Continue our amazing journey, together climb the hill

I think about where we are, what signs did I miss?
Because it's hard to believe that you wanted this

My Love For You

I'll leave the messages here
And hope that you will read
Of all the people in the world
Of anyone that I need

Why was it you
That touched my heart so well
Why does my love endure
When I hear you scream and yell?

My love for you, my dear,
Didn't happen overnight
It grew every day
It knew no wrong or right

But sometimes in life
It's not meant to be
You needed to move on
But this felt right to me

So I'll leave the messages here
Because this will have to do
And maybe you read them one day
And you'll feel my love for you!

Who Knows?

Who knows why you don't want me?
I guess I never will.
Who knows why I won't give up on us
And why I love you still?

Who knows where it went wrong?
Was it months, weeks, or days?
Who knows the exact time and place?
You've explained it so many ways.

Who knows if you'll want me again?
Will that love ever fill your heart?
Who knows if this is forever
Or just the summer we're apart?

Who knows why time goes so slow
And why minutes feel like days?
Who knows why the night doesn't come
And why now all I can do is pray?

Who knows why my prayers aren't answered
And why there's an empty space?
Who knows why you want your own life
And why I moved to my place?

So I move through time
just to see how it goes.
Will my prayers be answered today?
Who knows?

The Night Is the Hardest

I can get through the day, I can pass the test
But night is a different story, I can't find any rest

I toss and turn with each passing hour
Stare at the clock, my body drained of its power

I'll go on believing that this is all a dream
And I'll wake with a smile, so real it seems.

My tired body aches, and sweat pours out
I'm so mad sometimes I just want to shout

But who will listen alone in the stillness?
Who will be there, who'll be my witness?

I'll struggle with heartache all by myself
Place the booze way up on a higher shelf

Because it's tempting sometimes to just let loose
But doing that just becomes an excuse

I know my heart hurts, I'm not the smartest
So I close my eyes, and still the night is the hardest!

Will You Reply?

I can't ask you to respond
I can't ask you to reply
The only thing I can do
Is wonder if you read, if not, why?
I send an email
To tell you how I feel
And hope you understand
That what we have is so real
The other things
That you text me about
Are simply excuses in your mind
And each one creates doubt
But look to your heart
And listen to it closely
It shows you a path
That gets you back to me mostly
The rest has to come
From your feelings inside
And continue with me
On this most fantastic ride
It all starts for me
With a simple hi
And makes my heart sing
Whenever you reply!

No Reply

I write you a message
But don't expect a reply
I hope you read what I send
But don't expect you to cry

I certainly wish sometimes
That I could get a reaction
Just a message from you
Telling me about your attraction

Something in the words
That may trigger a feeling
Or a realization in you
That you want to start our healing

I'll be here, waiting for sure
As I've said a time or two
Because I have never felt
Anywhere near how I feel with you

But I send little messages
Or notes to ask, "Why?"
But instead of any answers
I simply expect no reply

You Are Beautiful

Are you looking for someone to tell you
You are beautiful every day?
Are you wanting someone to love you
In every word that they say?

Are you looking for someone special
That holds your hand at night?
Are you wanting a special person
That gets lightheaded at your sight?

Are you thinking you'll go out
And you'll find something so new?
Or will you find that certain someone
Whose love is 100 percent true?

You can go around this whole world
You can search this entire town
But that person you are seeking
The person that will never let you down

He's standing right in front of you
You don't have to go very far
To hear the words you want to hear
He'll tell you how beautiful you are!

Fast

Sometimes words come so fast
And other times not at all
But I want to keep writing to you
And hope my thoughts don't hit a wall

Will any of these words
Just fall into the right place?
Will one stand out to you
And put a big smile on your face?

Would you listen if I said the word
That brings you back to me?
Could you read that one phrase?
And it is precise to help you see

So whether these words I write
Come fast or slow
They are things I want to say to you
Just to let you know

You are never far from my thoughts
In everything that I do
I can't turn emotions off
Even if I wanted to

So I'll wait for something
Whether it's bad or good
And quickly write down words
To tell you I'd do it differently if I could

Traveling These Roads

I travel the same roads
I frequent the same places
I see all the same people
I know all their faces

But when I go home
At the end of the night
I'm not going to our house
I take a different path that doesn't feel right

No, I live in a gilded cage
My emotions won't let me be
The roads that I travel now
Are filled with memories of you and me

Funnily enough, my memories
Are great thoughts that make me smile
And I hope a day comes soon enough
When you don't let me travel another lonely mile

I suppose only time will tell
If that day will ever come
Can we love the same as we did?
If not fully at first, can you love me some?

We'll travel our roads again
We'll live life to the fullest
Bring back the trust and love
And you'll see our love is the purest

All I Hear

It's all I hear on the radio
The only songs I hear
Our songs all day long
Or ones that you hold dear

They are all simple reminders
Of a love that used to be
Each one a special meaning
When their stories talk to me

Each one tells a sad story
Of a precious love that was lost
A lonely life, a lot of missed chances
And a broken heart was the cost

All I hear are the voices
Telling me, "Forget her,
She wants to live a life without you
And you need to let her"

But no matter what words I hear
None will bring you back to me
So I'll listen to these words
"If you love someone, set them free

If they come back
You know the rest
And if they don't,
Then that's what's best!"

Sad Things

Sad things are everywhere
They're in everything I do
There are the silly things
That always remind of you

It might be a song
Or a place we would go
It could be a concert
Or maybe even a show

They are little reminders
Of the fun that we had
If you add everything up
You'd agree it wasn't all bad

More times than not
We'd always have a great time
No one ever had a doubt
That you were simply mine

After five years
You decided it wasn't enough
And that decision you made
Has been something for me so tough

We had beaten the odds
We had chosen each other
We had so much fun
That there was never time for another

But that time has passed
And you wanted to move on
I picked up and moved out
It seems your love had gone

I hope things change
Maybe a new song your heart sings
And we can continue on with our life
And quickly forget all these sad things

3:00 AM

Funny, all the thoughts I have at 3:00 AM
If only I could wake and remember them

In the middle of the night, they seem so real
I lie there and think it's exactly how I feel

In the morning, it's just a passing thought
Memories of a lost love that my heart caught

The thoughts linger as the day passes to night
I lay my head down, holding those memories tight

Hoping I feel the same next time I wake
Knowing those thoughts still make my heart ache

If only good thoughts could replace the bad
Waking at 3:00 AM wouldn't make me so sad

Happy for You

I'm glad you can wait this out
I'm happy that you think it helps
To think another weekend passes
And you're in the arms of someone else

I'm happy for you now
That you can move on with life
But for me, I'm stuck with my thoughts
Eventually, you'll be someone else's wife

I'll live with those thoughts
That I wasn't enough
And now someone else makes you happy
It's those thoughts that are tough

Maybe that day comes
When you've had all your fun
And you look back at us
And realize I was the one

The one who was there for you
The one who put you first
The one who loved you
Until his giant heart burst

I've said it all before
And I'll say it again
What we have is special
You'll never find it with other men

So I'll not give up
Because my love is true
And if you have given up
Well, then I'm happy for you

Your Time

I know you think that the feelings will pass
And for you, that may have happened fast

But for me, the feelings will always stay
Thoughts of you are with me night and day

All good thoughts of the love we shared
Our life together because we once dared

Did your feelings get pushed aside so quick?
Or is there love in your heart, a love that will stick?

Could you write to me just a note or a letter
To tell me everything will eventually be better?

Or maybe you had your time by yourself
And now you want a life with someone else

When that time comes, and we know it will
I hope it's me you choose as I love you still

So go out, live your life, and have fun
But it's you I want to see when my day is done

It's been months, but it could be years
I will not believe that this cost you so many tears

So many that you want a life without me
So many that now we live a life so lonely

Please come back and give this a try
Our life will be wonderful with no more goodbyes!

Missing You

There seems to be certain times in the night
Where I'll wake up and miss holding you tight

It's in those times that I miss you the most
Other times too, though, like FBag or The Post

I know you are done, I wasn't who you were looking for
But I think you're wrong and want a chance, just one more

This morning, I drove to the market, it was only me
My thought the whole time was all the things I wanted you to see

But you weren't next to me, you aren't even in the same state
You've decided to do trips with others, and that's the thought I hate

So I'll go on doing things by myself, it's really all I can do
The only other thing I know after all this? I'm still missing you!

Starting Over

Can you forgive my mistakes?
Can you overlook my faults?
Can we please start over?
Maybe if we try, the pain just halts

I understand all the trouble I caused
Talking too much to all the wrong friends
Asking questions, telling stories
Trusting I was right till the bitter end

If we can start over
Look to the future and not the past
I know mistakes were made
But we have a strong bond that can last

It's you I still want
At the end of each day
And to take on the world
No matter what comes our way

Now, though, it's my insecurities
Away they drove her
So all I can ask is for a date
So maybe we can then start over

Why?

Why do I still care
When clearly you don't?
Why do I still love you
When clearly you won't?

I know all the dumb sayings
I can't make someone love me
Or "If you love something, let it go
If it comes back, it was meant to be"

Why does the pain tear through me
Burning like dry leaves on a fall day?
Why does one see all the love shared
But the other sees it a different way?

No one has all the answers
Even when the right questions are asked
No one can take away the pain
You just have to let time pass

It seems that there is only one
That puts the blue back in the sky
But the days remain dark for now
And all I can ask is "Why?"

You're Everything

When I say that you're everything to me
It's just a feeling that won't let me be

You're in my thoughts both day and night
You visit my dreams and it feels so right

I see you everywhere when I go out
Two people laughing, that's us, no doubt

No matter where I look, you're always there
I see a couple holding hands and I just stare

Is that couple as happy as we once were?
Does she love him as much as he loves her?

Each one goes out and searches for the other
Once they meet, do they ever want another?

Do their eyes meet like ours used to?
And the world is right there's nothing to do

Do they know like me when their hearts start to sing?
Do they know in that moment that you are everything.

I Hear You

Believe me when I say
That I hear you loud and clear
But I think you're wrong
I think we are so near

We talk in your kitchen
And you tell me the issue
But you can't compare
A napkin to a tissue

We have love in our heart
We have a special connection
People would be happy for us
If we get back that love and affection

"I Prayed for You"
Is a song you sang to me
Listen to that once more
Hear the words so you see

I know you don't see
Us together in thirty years
But just look to the future
Without any trouble or tears

We can have that again
And there will be no trying
You have my heart
Until the day I'm dying

Please don't shut me out
Let's go on a date
And let me work on you
And turn your heart to love from hate

Connection

I sometimes drive by our house
Just to feel that connection
I look for you on the street
Because my life has no direction

I will never believe
That I wasn't enough
That our time together
For you was so rough

We had each other's backs
We were a special pair
No matter what we did
We had our connection anywhere

That connection was disrupted
A short circuit in the wires
You wanted a break
I wasn't what your heart desires

So you wonder why I care
Why I want so badly the connection
You are the best thing that's happened
I want your love and your affection

That's Not You

Hanging out at the bars
Because there's nothing else to do
The last time I checked
That certainly wasn't you

Driving a car and riding a bike
I'm sure you would choose neither
Maybe forgiving someone's mistake
Pretty sure you wouldn't do that either

Denying a love
Simply basing it on principle
Living separate lives
Thinking that is permissible

I could list more things
And say that's not you
But as time goes on
I'm not sure that I want to

I want to simply list
What I know in my heart
That maybe you're miserable
And really hating our time apart

Not a Care

I imagine your day
Filled with excitement and fun
Not a care in the world
Your freedom you won

Too busy with life
To have a thought about me
Too much fun to be had
Living life so carefree

No one at your empty house
To question your decisions
No one to come home to
That's how I envision

Sometimes I lie here
And wish you did have a care
And wanted to talk about us
Take that chance if you dare

Maybe the day comes
When you don't want a house so empty
If you call me on that day
I will be there, so please tempt me

Yesterday Is Gone

There's a reason people sing the way they do
Each song tells a story of me and you

Songs filled with love and filled with loss
They tell of fun times followed by a high cost

Some sing about going back to yesterday
But sometimes it's really hard to find the way

Lovers get lost in thinking of all the bad
And forget about all the great times they had

If I could wish just one thing for us
Concentrating on the good is definitely a must

You know mistakes will always be made
But the underlying love does not fade

I have one hope when I wake this next dawn
I hope it's not true that yesterday is gone

Found the One

I found the one with whom to travel these paths
The one who made my life complete
I found the one who made me smile
The one who I just had to meet

She taught me to live to the fullest
And understand how life can be
It was fun and exciting to see the world
A partner for life to run around with me

It was years in the making
To find that special one
It took a long time to find her
Many trips around the sun

Then, like the wind, she was gone
Moved on to do others things
For as full as my heart felt
Today it's sad songs that it sings

Will she ever come back to me?
How many more trips around the sun
Until she either is back in my arms
Or tells me she's found another one?

I'll wait for as long as it takes
Because I know the love that is there
I just need her to see it also
See it clearly, the love we share

One Hundred Poems

I'll close this book now
With one hundred poems written
Words that tell a story
Of a boy that was bitten

Bitten by that special love
That makes you fall hard
A story of love and loss
That blindly moves without regard

No regard for anything
It just follows its own road
A love that only goes faster
Through the years, it hasn't slowed

It hasn't slowed for the boy
It showed him how a love can be
A life that finally felt complete
Eyes opened wide so he could see

He could see that with the right person
Life could simply be fun
Just move through this life
Knowing that you're with the right one

The right one who's special
And feels exactly right
A person who makes you happy
And whom you want to hold all night

But these poems for now
Will simply have to do
And maybe they'll be read one day
And you'll feel my love pouring through!

About the Author

Dan has lived in St. Louis for most of his life but moved away for nine years to live in Springfield, Missouri, to attend school and, after, became a bar owner. Currently he is a mortgage loan officer during the day but enjoys traveling and visiting with his two grown sons. Dan also runs trivia nights for charities and is the social director of a local pool where he is a member. The book was inspired by a rough time in his life, and it was a way to deal with the sorrow. While this is his first time publishing a book, he will attempt more in the future.

www.ingramcontent.com/pod-product-compliance
Lightning Source LLC
Chambersburg PA
CBHW032311120125
20280CB00010B/487